NICOTEXT

The Bar & Pub
Truth or Dare

Copyright © NICOTEXT 2012 All rights reserved.
NICOTEXT part of Cladd media Ltd.
www.nicotext.com
info@nicotext.com

Printed in Poland
ISBN: 978-91-86283-74-2

DO NOT DRINK AND DRIVE & DO NOT DRINK ALCOHOL
IF YOU ARE UNDER DRINKING AGE!

...AND KIDS, REMEMBER, ALWAYS WEAR A CONDOM!

Rules:

Truth or Dare is a piece of cake. But it's a bit trickier when you are in a public place.

Bring this book to a bar and challenge your friends.
You'll probably also make new friends, and perhaps even go to jail. Either way, you'll have fun.

This is how it's done:

• First decide on Truth or Dare.

• Flip through the pages until you feel like stopping, but no reading before you do!

Rules:

• **Alternatively; simply say a number between 8 and 207, even numbers are Dares and odd numbers Truths.**

There shall be no lying, cheating or otherwise avoiding embarrassing questions and dares. Know this, he or she who tries will be severly punished by the great Leprechaun of the Black Forrest in the East.
A most uncomfortable experience, we assure you.

Dare

Decide on a person in the bar. Everyone in your group guesses his or her name. Find out, and whoever comes closest shall receive a jolly good award.

Truth

If you had to choose a new sex partner in this bar, right now, who would you pick?

9

Dare

Find someone with untied shoe laces.
Offer them to solve the problem.

10

If you were invisible within this bar only, what would be the first thing you would do?

11

Dare

Choose a couple of guests further away and imagine out loud to your friends who they are and what they are talking about.

12

When was the last time you
changed your sheets?

Dare

Take seven steps. Start talking to the person you now stand closest to.

14

Truth

On this fine evening, who is the best looking of your co-players?

15

Dare

Find someone dressed in black.
Invite that person to go and
see the stars with you.

16

What's the strangest sex position you've ever tried?

Dare

Send a Shirley Temple to a person standing at the bar.

18

What's the most stupid thing you've ever done when drunk?

Dare

Get eye contact and flirt with a person that you have never seen before.

20

Which of your physical attributes
do you get the most compliments for?

21

Dare

Guess the bartenders favourite drink. See if you are right.

22

Truth

Describe your worst fashion disaster.

23

Dare

Get everyone a glass of water – your treat!

24

Truth

Which two would be the oddest
love couple in this room?
Why?

25

Dare

Find someone with a good hair day.
Compliment them on their hairdo.

26

Have you ever seen anyone
in this room naked?
Who and when?

Dare

Propose a toast for the co-player you think made most progress in any area today.

28

Describe the last porn movie you saw.

Dare

Let your co-players send a text from your phone to the person you made your last phone call to.

30

Have you ever had an STD?
Who gave it to you?

Dare

Gather your forces and form a queue to the toilet. Everyone must go!

Have you ever broken any laws?
Which ones?

Dare

Ask someone in the bar to go for a coffee with you tomorrow.

34

Have you ever had a friends-with-benefits relationship with anyone? With whom and how did it work out?

35

Dare

Propose to one very lucky person in this room, on one knee!

36

Who would you vote for if there
was an election today?

Dare

Find someone with a funny-looking drink in his or her hand. Ask them what it is called and order the same one.

Among your co-players, who are most likely to be famous in the future?

39

Dare

Sing happy b-day for a random person in the bar. Get everyone to sing along with you.

40

Name five deal-breakers in a relationship.

Dare

Give a random person a hickey.

42

Truth

How often do you masturbate? Let your co-players guess before you answer this question.

43

Dare

Guess who's the horniest person in the bar.

44

Who would you love to make out with in this room?

Dare

Let your best friend on the premises decide on one new person you should make out with tonight.

46

Are there any nude pictures of you?
Who took them and how
are you posing?

47

Dare

Find someone who looks like they have the same taste in music as you do. Find out if you are right.

48

What drugs have you tried?

Dare

Sing a song for someone and have them guess what song you're singing.

50

How do you like to be seduced?

Dare

Ask someone to join you and
your friends for a toast.

52

Do you have sex on the first date?

Dare

Find the best looking tattoo in the bar.

54

What's the worst date you've
ever been on?

Dare

Arm-wrestle the person to your right.

56

Who's the meanest friend you've ever had?

Dare

Whisper something to the person at the right end of the bar. Ask them to whisper the same thing to the person to their left. Encourage every new person to keep whispering. Follow the whisper through the whole bar and then ask the last person to say it out loud.

58

Who in this bar are you afraid of the most? Why?

Dare

Let your friends decide who you should talk to. Walk up to the chosen person and ask him or her what they think about kittens.

60

What are the most annoying things about each of your co-players?

Dare

Spin around ten times and then walk 5 steps straight forward. Ask the first person you see for a dance.

62

How do you pick someone up?
Describe it in words.

63

Dare

For the next 15 minutes, kiss everyone that makes eye contact with you on the cheek.

Among your co-players, who's the horniest one?

Dare

Give five people you don't know a compliment.

Truth

Tell your co-players of your wildest night out.

67

Dare

Kiss one other player on the mouth.

68

Truth

Tell your co-players of a near-death-experience you've had.

69

Dare

Collect tips from everyone and give it to your favourite bartender.

70

Have you ever been on a blind date?
How did it go?

71

Dare

Go and flirt with someone who's obviously busy with another conversation.

72

What bodily fluids have you tasted?

73

Dare

Make a flower out of a napkin and give it to the most beautiful person in the bar.

74

What's the kinkiest thing you've done during sex?

Dare

Find someone with dimples.
Make them show.

76

Have you ever gotten a DUI?
Have you ever driven drunk?

Dare

Let a person at one table over write something on your arm.

78

How long did your longest
sex session last?

Dare

Find someone with mismatched socks.

80

What's the most expensive thing you've shoplifted?

Dare

Order nuts and give them to someone while telling them that "I'm nuts for you!" Then you may leave.

82

Have you been thrown out of a bar/club? Why?

Dare

Run once around the block.

84

What's the worst relationship
you've ever been in?

Dare

Imitate one of the other players.
Let everyone guess who you are.

86

Truth

Name something you're jealous of, of each of your co-players.

87

Dare

Ask the bartender to make his or her most special drink for you.

88

When did you last experience a "walk of shame"?

Dare

All players must change at least one garment with one of the other players. Everyone should wear something new once you're done.

90

Have you ever faked an orgasm?
What was the reason?

Dare

Finish the drink belonging to the person on your left.

92

Truth

Tell your co-players of an embarrassing text that you've sent to the wrong person.

93

Dare

Offer a cute stranger a great back massage.

94

At what occasion were you the closest to living like a rock star?

Dare

Let the person on your right post something on your Facebook wall.

Among your co-players, who has the dirtiest mind?

Dare

Organize a burping contest.

98

When was the last time you had
unprotected sex?

99

Dare

Let the player on the left write a booty text on your phone. You have to send it to someone in your phone book but you decide to whom.

100

What is the worst way in which you've ended a relationship?

Dare

Get the doormans` or the bartenders` number.

102

When did you make a fool out
of yourself in a sexual situation?

Dare

Get out on a pretend catwalk
and show your stuff.

104

Which birthday was your best one ever so far?

Dare

Give the person to your right an everlasting hug.

106

Have you ever blurted out the wrong name while having sex?

107

Dare

Do the robot dance.

Do you keep a list over your sex partners?
How many are there?

Dare

Order something you've never tried before.

110

Truth

Who was the last person you had sex with?
Do tell details.

111

Dare

Kiss the hand of the person who you admire the most in this room.

112

Who is the most criminal person you know?

Dare

Buy a drink for a person you don't know.

114

Who would you play in a porn movie?

Dare

Ask the bartender for his/her name. Use it proportionate but fairly often during the night.

116

Who do you feel sorry for in this room? Why?

117

Dare

Go to the toilet and change all your clothes (except underwear) with a co-player of your choice.

What fetish interests you?

Dare

Give all players a kiss on their lips.

120

Truth

Who have you lied to the most
in this room?

121

Dare

Take a walk around the room and make eye contact with at least five people you don't know from before. Look them in the eye until they turn their gaze.

122

When were you latest in a serious fight?
What was it about?

123

Dare

Correct the other players' speech for the next two minutes.

124

What's the latest gossip you've helped spread? About whom?

125

Dare

Bottoms up.

126

Truth

When did you lie about your age recently?

127

Dare

Pretend that you are a priest and bless this holy evening. Use at least five swwear words in your sermon.

128

Truth

Tell your co-players about a sexual fantasy you have.

129

Dare

Everyone should call someone and let that person know how much he or she loves them.

Tell every co-player about his or her best personal quality.

131

Dare

Try to get the hiccups. Really try.

132

Who made a real bad choice of outfit this evening?

133

Dare

Make someone an offer they can't refuse!

Have you ever woken up naked without knowing where you were?

135

Dare

Make a comment about each
of your co-players outfits.
Good or bad.

136

Who has the most annoying habit in this room?

Dare

Open a door or a window and scream:
"I'm a monster and you're my prey!".

Order the co-players names from smartest to dumbest.

Dare

Pretend you're reading the mind of the player on your left. Tell everyone what he or she is thinking.

140

What's the craziest decision
you've ever made?

Dare

Use a pick-up line to start a conversation with a stranger.

142

What day of your life do you
regret the most?

Dare

Ask a stranger if YOU are here often.

144

Among your co-players, who do you think is the kinkiest? Why?

145

Dare

Decide on a song that illustrates this evening. Sing it together.

Who do you really regret breaking up with?

Dare

Try to seduce a co-player of the same sex.

148

What do your co-players brag about?
Name one thing per person.

149

Dare

Change socks with a stranger at the bar.

150

Who's the bitchiest person in this room?

Dare

Let the person on your right mess up your hair.

152

Who in this bar do you think will get laid tonight?

Dare

Inspect all your co-players photo IDs.

154

Among your co-players,
who kisses ass the most?

Dare

Ask the cutest person in the room
for a slow dance.

Truth

Which of your co-players are you most
likely to have sex with? Why?

157

Dare

Ask a stranger if his or her father is a criminal. Then reveal that you own father is one.

158

Insult each co-player in a brutal way with a painful truth.

159

Dare

Next time you visit the bathroom you should start a conversation in the line about leprechauns.

Have you ever starved yourself to loose weight? What's the worst diet you have ever tried?

161

Dare

Find a lipstick and make all players wear some.

162

What does your sexiest
outfit look like?

Dare

Drink something without using your arms.

Did you ever beg for someone to take you back? How have you humiliated yourself the most in a love relationship?

Dare

Challenge a random person to a staring contest; the one that starts laughing first loses.

What has been the best sex in your life so far? When and with whom? Why was it soooo damn good then?

167

Dare

Be a psychic and give everyone his or her fortune for the night.

Who is the most famous person you've dated or kissed?

Dare

Smell everyone's breath and tell who's in most desperate need of a toothbrush.

170

What do you call your intimate parts?

171

Dare

Call someone and claim you've been
kidnapped. Really convince them.

What's the worst smell you've ever experienced?

Dare

Let the guards body search you. If they already did, tell them that you think they missed something.

174

What kind of forbidden love
have you experienced?

175

Dare

Ask someone to take a group photo of yourself and your friends. Everyone must be in it.

Truth

Have you ever been unfaithful?
If not: what's the closest
you've come?

177

Dare

Stand on one leg for five minutes.

178

What is your favourite sex position?

Dare

Change your dialect and talk with another accent for 15 minutes.

180

Have you ever had phone sex? With whom and how did the conversation go?

Dare

Time stands still. Arrange all your co-players in situations you want them to be in and start time again.

Truth

Let every co-player ask you an intimate question.

183

Dare

Find someone wearing the colour red.
Ask that person for his or her star sign.

184

What are you really insecure about right now?

Dare

Speak with a babies voice until it's your turn again.

Who is most likely to become an alcoholic in this bar?

Dare

Let the other players decide on one person each that you must talk to during the evening.

188

What is the most dangerous situation
you have put yourself in?

Dare

Feel your co-players ass and decide who's got the best one.

190

Which of your co-players family members would you consider sleeping with?

Dare

Give every co-player your sluttiness rating.

192

Point out one person in this room that is better looking than you are.

Dare

Find the person with the nicest shoes in the bar and compliment him/her.

What are your prejudices?
Name three things.

Dare

Give the other players a memorable
lesson about the birds and the bees.
Use at least two objects to illustrate
what you're describing.

196

What is your most disgusting habit?

Dare

Describe each player with one sexy adjective.

Would you pay for sex if that was the only way to get it for the rest of your life?

Dare

Make up a new handshake with your fellow companions.

200

Tell everyone in your group what the first impression of him or her was.

201

Dare

Give a nice gift to the person three steps to your right.

202

When was the last time you lied?
About what?

Dare

Find someone with a good sense of humour.
Tell that person your best joke ever.

204

Truth

When it comes to picking someone up, who one of your co-players do you think is the smoothest?

205

Dare

Make a speech praising one of
the other players.

206

If you had to guess, who is the sluttiest person in this room?

207